No More Bedtime Battles

SIMPLE SOLUTIONS TO BEDTIME PROBLEMS

Lee Canter and Marlene Canter

Effective Parenting Books

Contributing Writers
Patricia Sarka
Marcia Shank

Book Design
Joyce Vario

Cover Art and Design
Richard Rossiter

Editorial Staff
Marlene Canter
Carol Provisor
Barbara Schadlow
Kathy Winberry

© 1996 Lee Canter & Associates
P.O. Box 2113, Santa Monica, CA 90407-2113
800-262-4347   310-395-3221

Printed in the United States of America
First printing April 1996
00 99 98 97 96   10 9 8 7 6 5 4 3 2 1

ISBN #0-939007-78-9

Problems in Slumberland?

BEATING THE BEDTIME BLUES

Do these statements sound familiar? If so, read on.

You've had another tough day. Up early. Work all day. Shop for groceries. Pick up your child at the babysitter's. Make dinner. Pick up kids from the dance. Chat with the family. Help with homework. Write the bills.

Then, when it's time to put your child to bed a new battle begins:

"Please let me stay up just five more minutes!"

"Why do I have to go to bed? Jason gets to stay up later."

"Let me watch just one more program."

And once you do get your child into bed, you hear:

"I'm not sleepy. Read me another story!"

"I'm scared. There's a monster in my bedroom."

"I want to sleep in your bed."

If these bedtime scenarios have a familiar ring, you're not alone. Most parents have difficulty at one time or another getting their children to bed—and keeping them there. And when a child has bedtime problems, parents are affected as well.

Few things are as frustrating as arguing with your child at the end of a long day about getting to bed on time.

Few things are as annoying as hassling with a tired child in the morning because she stayed up too late the night before watching TV.

And few things are as unnerving as the first whimper of a child who was awakened in the night, frightened by a dream or of benign shadows in the bedroom.

Don't be discouraged! You can beat these bedtime blues. By using the simple suggestions in this book, bedtime can become a pleasant experience for your child and a relaxing end to the day for you.

Bedtime

IT SHOULD BE THE PERFECT ENDING TO THE DAY

Evenings should be a time when families wind down from the busy day, share experiences, and enjoy pleasant nighttime activities and conversation together before settling down to a restful night's sleep. But for many families, evenings are anything but a nice time of day. Instead, they are filled to capacity with the hustle-bustle of dinner, dishes, homework, housework and children fighting for the TV remote, their parents' attention and the biggest slice of chocolate cake. Everyone is rushed. Time flies by. And before you know it, bedtime has come and gone. With a harried glance at the clock, parents speed children off to bed with a peck on the cheek and a quick-but-not-too-emphatic reminder to brush their teeth.

What happens when bedtime isn't given the attention it deserves? Plenty!

- A child doesn't have adequate time to make a gradual transition from the excitement of the day's activities to the relaxation necessary for falling asleep and staying asleep.

- A child doesn't have adequate time for good personal hygiene (bathing, washing hair, brushing and flossing).

- Attention isn't given to getting ready for the next day—planning what to wear, putting homework where it will be remembered in the morning, and taking care of the odds and ends that otherwise end up causing stress and unnecessary problems the next day.

- And, most importantly, both parent and child lose a wonderful opportunity to spend special quiet time together at bedtime—talking, reading, and sharing thoughts about the day just passed and the one to come.

Results?

Bedtime battles, frayed nerves, and an unsatisfying end to the day—for you and your chid.

Relax!

You don't have to have a hectic, rushed evening— and you don't have to miss out on these important, special bedtime moments. The key to a better bedtime is in planning your child's bedtime routine.

What is a bedtime routine?

A bedtime routine is a sequence of events your child follows each evening to prepare for bed and sleep. Although specific bedtime routines will vary from family to family, those that are most successful at helping children calm down, prepare for bed, get in bed and stay in bed have these elements in common:

- The bedtime routine is followed **consistently**.
- **Adequate time** is allowed for getting-ready-for-bed activities.
- Child and parent share **special, one-to-one time together**—every night.
- Bedtime conversations are **positive and reassuring**.

For example, a good bedtime routine might last 45 minutes and include these activities:

1. Take a warm bath.
2. Brush teeth.
3. Put on pajamas.
4. Lay out school clothes for tomorrow.
5. Say goodnight to family members.
6. Listen to parent read a favorite story.
7. Talk with parent about the day at school.
8. Discuss plans for tomorrow.
9. Share hugs and kisses.
10. Turn out the light and go to sleep.

The child who follows this routine each night will have adequate time to relax, clean up, prepare for the next day and spend special time with a parent. The perfect prescription for a better sleep and a better tomorrow!

How is bedtime handled now in your family? Does your child have a routine? If your answer is yes, how is the routine working?

If bedtime battles are part of your typical evening, read on. There are answers.

What Time Is Bedtime?

A GOOD PLACE TO START

How much sleep do you want your child to get? How much sleep is adequate? The amount of sleep needed depends on the age and sleep requirements of the child.

Here are some typical sleep requirements of children:

Birth to 1 year	13–16 hours (including naps)
2–5 years	11–13 hours (including naps)
6–9 years	10–11 hours
10–18 years	8–10 hours

These are, of course, only guidelines. It's important to remember that you are the best judge of how much sleep your child needs to be at his or her best during the day. If your child gets cranky during the day, he may not be getting enough sleep. If your child complains of being tired upon waking in the morning, and is still tired after five or ten minutes, then she is getting to bed too late. Time to readjust bedtime.

Is your child getting enough sleep?

A helpful way to determine if your child is getting all the sleep he needs is to chart bedtimes and wake-up times in a 2-Week Sleep Diary. Use the Sleep Diary on pages 63–64 to record your child's sleep habits over a two-week period. Here's how:

- On the first morning, write the time your child awakens. Make note of your child's attitude after the first ten minutes: happy, cooperative, whiny, tired, irritable.

- If your child takes naps, record these in the Sleep Diary too. Write the time and duration of the nap.

- If your child doesn't take naps, but appears fatigued, weary or just plain tuckered out during the day, note the time in the Day 1 box.

- At day's end, write the time your child goes to sleep.

- If your child had a "good day," put a star in the box.

- Follow the same procedure for a week or two. When you've completed the Sleep Diary, take note of the "star" days and the times your child went to sleep those days. This is a good indicator of a bedtime that works for your child.
- Look also at activities that occur on certain days. Days that include more strenuous pastimes may require an earlier bedtime the night before.

Once you've decided when you want your child to go to bed, it's time to turn your attention to planning a routine that will have your child tucked in on time, relaxed and happily prepared for the day to come.

The Bedtime Hour

The Bedtime Hour is a special time each night set aside for moving your child from the activities of the day to going to sleep.

The Bedtime Hour may be 15 minutes, or it may be an hour. The length of time doesn't matter. What does matter is that each night during the Bedtime Hour you and your child will follow a consistent, pleasant routine that will ensure that what needs to be done each night will be done, and, most important, that you and your child are able to share special one-to-one time together.

Is this bedtime routine really that important?

Yes! Children find comfort in items and activities that are familiar and repetitious. Carrying a special blanket, hugging a worn but beloved stuffed animal or listening to a familiar story can provide a young child with a comforting sense of security. Even older children find reassurance in wearing favorite pajamas or having a childhood quilt on the bed.

A regular bedtime routine provides children with that same kind of comfort, security and predictability. Most people don't like surprises, and children are no different. They like to know exactly what will happen next—especially at bedtime.

A bedtime routine helps children know exactly what they are to do before bed.

Developing and sticking to a bedtime routine will provide your child with the comfortable, secure atmosphere that makes going to bed a pleasant experience, and thus will increase the likelihood that your child will sleep contentedly through the night.

> *"When it's bedtime, I take a bath, brush my teeth, pick out my clothes for tomorrow, choose a book for Mom to read to me, crawl into bed, hear my story, give Mom a hug and kiss, turn out the light and go to sleep."*

> *"When it's time to go to bed, I take a shower, brush and floss, pack my lunch, choose my clothes for tomorrow, talk things over with my parents for a few minutes, say goodnight, read for 15 minutes, turn out the light and go to sleep."*

As you continue to read through this book, and plan your own child's Bedtime Hour, make a commitment to follow through with the routine each and every night. In no time, your child's bedtime problems will be history.

The Bedtime Hour

A 3-STEP PLAN

To help you plan your child's nighttime routine, we've broken the Bedtime Hour into three parts:

1. **Nightly Hygiene**

   Bathing, washing, brushing and flossing

2. **Planning for Tomorrow**

   Selecting clothes, packing up homework

3. **Parent-Child Time**

   Reading together, sharing thoughts, talking about the day

On the pages that follow, you will learn how to create a bedtime routine for your child that includes each of these important areas.

STEP

1

The Bedtime Hour

NIGHTLY HYGIENE

Part of growing up healthy is learning to develop good hygiene habits. And part of going to bed happy, relaxed and feeling good is being clean, scrubbed and groomed. It's important that children develop these habits when they are young, and that these habits are encouraged and reinforced as they grow older.

A nightly personal hygiene routine is an important part of any child's Bedtime Hour. Not only will your child be clean for the next day, but he or she will also learn to take responsibility for personal grooming habits.

Establish your child's personal grooming routine.

Get your child into the habit of following a step-by-step hygiene routine every night. Use the Bedtime Hour Chart on pages 65–66 to list the hygiene activities that will be part of your child's nightly going-to-bed routine.

BEDTIME HOUR Chart

Bedtime: _____

Your bedtime routine will be:

NIGHTLY HYGIENE
1. _____
2. _____
3. _____
4. _____
5. _____
6. _____

PLANNING FOR TOMORROW
1. _____
2. _____
3. _____
4. _____
5. _____
6. _____

PARENT-CHILD TIME
We'll spend some time together each night.

_____
Parent Signature

Here is a sample of a nightly hygiene routine:

- Take bath
- Brush teeth
- Floss teeth
- Brush hair

Don't rush your child! Allow ample time for a relaxing bath, shower, or wash-up at the sink, a thorough teeth cleaning, and any hygiene extras your child needs to take care of.

Personal grooming should be a pleasant pastime that helps your child wind down from the day—not something to be hurried through and done poorly.

The Bedtime Hour

PLANNING FOR TOMORROW

As any parent can attest, mornings are often every bit as hectic as evenings as children search the house for lost socks and misplaced homework, Mom tries to iron a wrinkled Scout uniform, and everyone belatedly discovers that there's no bread for lunch sandwiches. Take a break from this stress by doing a little advance planning the night before. Your child will start the next day on a better foot, and so will you.

Decide what activities can be planned the night before.

For example:

Set out tomorrow's clothes.

One of the biggest morning hassles is making last-minute clothing choices—and then discovering that everything's dirty. Avoid the tears and arguments!

Have your child plan what to wear the night before, when there's plenty of time to evaluate what will be the perfect ensemble for the next day. And don't forget to keep an eye on the weather forecast and special activities.

> *"The forecast calls for rain tomorrow and you've got your Scout meeting, so remember to put your rainboots next to your uniform."*

Older children can make their own clothing choices; younger children will need to be guided by you.

Gather school materials.

Before your child goes to bed, all school materials (homework, signed notes, library books, lunch money, etc.) should be put in a special place where they will be easy to retrieve the following morning. Toddlers and preschoolers can select special toys for daycare or preschool, too.

Prepare lunches.

Older children can prepare their own lunches the night before. Even little ones can help bagging fruit and sandwiches.

Continue using the Bedtime Hour Chart to list your child's "planning for tomorrow" activities. For example:

- Choose clothes.
- Put homework by the door.
- Prepare my lunch.

The Bedtime Hour

PARENT-CHILD TIME

Every child, from infant to teen, enjoys special one-to-one time with a parent before nodding off to sleep. This Parent-Child Time may be the first opportunity in an otherwise hectic and overscheduled day that parents have to devote to their children. Don't let it slip by.

Plan approximately how much time you will spend together.

How much time you spend with your child during Parent-Child Time depends on the time you have available. (If you have more than one child to tuck in at night, you will have to take that into consideration.) Ten or fifteen minutes can be the perfect allotment for a quiet conversation, a short story, and a kiss and hug goodnight. But you don't have to limit yourself to this time frame. Nightly reading of a good story may lend itself to a half-hour or more. And you don't want to cut off important conversations just to "stay on schedule."

Parent-Child Time should be a pleasant end to the day.

Here are some ideas for what to do:

✔ Help your child **look back on the day with positive feelings**. Encourage your child to think about the day that just passed by talking about the best thing that happened.

✔ **Set the stage for a good tomorrow** by discussing the upcoming day. Talk about something positive your child can look forward to.

> *"Tomorrow morning is pancake day."*
>
> *"We get our vacation photos back tomorrow. I can't wait to see the picture of you on skis."*
>
> *"You must really be looking forward to Sports Day tomorrow at school!"*

✔ **Read a bedtime story** or several nursery rhymes to your child. (No scary stories, please!)

✔ **Sing** to your child. Lullabies have been lulling children to sleep for centuries, but contemporary songs win approval, too!

✔ **Turn on soothing music** or a tape containing the comforting sounds of nature (raindrops, ocean).

✔ **Listen to a taped story** together.

✔ **Introduce your child to poetry** by reading poems from a book of children's verse. These nightly readings will help your child develop an appreciation of poetry and allow the two of you to explore many subjects and themes together.

✔ **Play a quiet game together** (Lego, Old Maid, Concentration).

✔ **Give your child a relaxing back, neck or foot massage** while sharing your favorite memories of his or her milestones (her first tooth, his first step, her first words, his first haircut).

✔ **Encourage your child to keep a diary or journal.** If your child is too young to write, invite a discussion about what happened during the day and write these comments, verbatim, in a notebook or diary. If your child has a computer, urge the development of an electronic diary.

Now complete your Bedtime Hour Chart by signing "Mom" or "Dad" (or both) in the space at the bottom. Fill in your child's bedtime at the top and show the chart to your child. Explain that in order to have a better evening and nightime, your child—and you— will be following these steps leading to bedtime. Read through the steps together and answer any questions your child may ask.

End every day with love and affection.

Although every day may be far from perfect, every day should have a perfect ending—sharing a special tradition of love and affection. A hug, a kiss and a heartfelt "I love you" should be part of every nightly routine. Even after a problem-filled day, your child must go to sleep with this reassurance of your love and devotion.

A Successful Bedtime Hour

TIPS FOR GETTING PAST THE ROADBLOCKS

Planning your child's nighttime routine will help make the Bedtime Hour a far more pleasant event for everyone. But there still of course will be times when your child won't settle down, can't get to sleep, and just can't seem to make a peaceful transition from day to night.

Here are some ideas that will help you get past these bedtime roadblocks.

Help your child get to bed on time.

Once you set a bedtime, stick to it! These tips will help.

Use a "Good Night" Chart.

Give your child extra incentive to get to bed on time by using a Good Night Chart. Post the chart (see pages 67–68) in your child's room. Each night he or she gets to bed on time, draw a star on the chart. When your child earns several stars, reward these super bedtime habits with a special privilege or surprise.

Try to keep daily bedtime in force even when you're away from home for the evening. Ask relatives and babysitters to use the chart when you're not there.

GOOD NIGHT!
Chart

WHEN I EARN _____ STARS,

I WILL RECEIVE _____.

Parents: Every night that your child behaves appropriately, draw a star on the chart. Younger children earn the reward in a few days, older children in one week. A special reward may also be earned after receiving a specified number of stars in a month.

Set a reasonable weekend bedtime.

It's best not to vary weekend bedtimes by more than an hour (except on very special occasions). Child "jet lag" can carry over into the next few days, making weekday bedtime problems more likely. This is especially important for children who have to get up and go to school on Monday mornings.

Don't negotiate bedtimes.

"Please can't I stay up late just tonight?" Unless it's a special occasion, stay firm! Once you give in, you'll set yourself up for an argument every night.

Be flexible under certain circumstances.

Don't be overly strict about bedtimes if special situations arise—relatives visiting from out of town, once-in-a-lifetime eclipse of the moon, Aunt Nell appearing as a contestant on a television game show. Some moments just can't be recaptured, and memories are the building blocks of your child's future.

Ease your child toward bedtime with a wind-down time.

If you want your child's Bedtime Hour to be relaxing and calm, encourage him to slow down and take it easy before the bedtime routine begins. Here are suggestions for making wind-down time the perfect bridge from the day's activities to the Bedtime Hour:

Do

✔ Do signal your child that the countdown to the Bedtime Hour has begun. You might say, "It's 8:00. In thirty minutes it will be time to start getting ready for bed." Or set an oven timer for thirty minutes and announce that when the timer rings, the bedtime ritual begins. This signal will give your child the opportunity to finish any activities he or she is involved in.

✔ Do encourage your child to switch from vigorous activities to ones that are calming and quiet as the Bedtime Hour draws closer. For example:

– Reading

– Listening to a taped story

– Looking through magazines, picture books, scrapbooks

– Working on a jigsaw puzzle

✔ Do guide your child toward doing homework earlier in the evening whenever possible. Schoolwork can be stressful, and studying for tests or drilling math problems can leave your child tense and concerned—conditions that are not conducive to sleep.

✔ Do limit video-game play to earlier in the evening. Some games can overstimulate your child to the point of interfering with the relaxation necessary to fall asleep.

Don't

✔ Don't wait until bedtime to reprimand your child or discuss family problems. Sleep doesn't come easily to a child who is upset or worried. The time just before bed is best used for soothing, pleasant conversation that leaves your child feeling good about himself and his place in the family.

✔ Don't encourage roughhousing, pillow fights, or any rambunctious behavior that will set your child's pulse racing.

✔ Don't allow television programs that may get your child too excited, agitated or upset. A movie-of-the-week on kidnapping isn't a wise lead-in to a blissful night's sleep.

✔ Don't let your child go to sleep without hearing loving words from you—a wonderful end-of-the-day gift to a child of any age.

Teach your child how to relax and fall asleep.

Children sometimes have difficulty falling asleep—just like adults. They may be anxious about the upcoming day—big baseball game, problems with a friend, holiday party at school. Their minds start racing the minute lights go out. By learning how to relax, your child will be able to fall asleep more easily. Most relaxation techniques involve focusing intently on something special, thus crowding out any "sleep-stealing thoughts" and allowing the child to fall asleep.

Introduce the "Eyes, Nose, Knees, Toes" Relaxation Method.

This is a simple technique to help your child systematically relax his or her muscles in preparation for sleep. Practice this "relaxing game" for a few minutes each evening before turning out your child's light. In no time, your child will be able to use the skill to relax not only at bedtime, but anytime during the day when things get a bit tense. Here's how:

1. Have your child lie comfortably on his or her back, eyes closed.

2. Direct your child by saying in a soft voice, "Scrunch up your entire face just as if you had taken a bite from a very sour lemon." Have your child hold this expression for five seconds and then quickly relax every muscle in the face. With eyes

still closed, ask your child to picture a soft breeze washing over the face. (You may want to gently stroke your hand down your child's face several times.)

3. Continue by saying, "Now clench your hands into tight fists and tighten all the muscles in your arms so that they are as stiff as boards." Have your child tense the arms for five seconds and then quickly relax every muscle from the shoulders down to the tips of the fingers. With eyes still closed, ask your child to picture a soft breeze washing over the face and arms. (You may want to gently stroke your hand down your child's face and arms several times.)

4. Now say, "Stiffen your legs and pull your toes back towards your head." Have your child continue this for five seconds and then quickly relax every muscle from the hips to the tips of the toes. With eyes still closed, ask your child to picture a soft breeze washing over the face, arms and legs. (You may want to gently stroke your hand down your child's face and arms several times.)

5. Then repeat in a soft voice, "Relax, eyes. Relax, nose, Relax, knees. Relax, toes." Continue repeating the phrase in a gradually quieter voice until the words are at a whisper.

Repeat this relaxation technique every night. Depending on your child's age, he or she should be able to practice this calming procedure in a week or two without your assistance.

Calm nighttime anxieties with a "Bedside Buddy Box."

You can put your child to bed, you can turn out the lights, but you can't make her go to sleep.

When your child calls out to you after going to bed, it is usually an attempt to get your attention. If this happens with your child, ask yourself, "Am I spending enough time with her during Parent-Child Time?" If children feel you are rushing through the Bedtime Hour just so that you can be alone at the end of the day, they may unconsciously rebel by calling out to you or getting out of bed. The best way to end this behavior is to give your child that attention during the Bedtime Hour.

If, however, you feel that this isn't the case, try this idea: Create a Bedside Buddy Box and fill it with those items your child frequently requests, or items that might help him or her relax. These items could include things your child feels he needs, or items that will provide comfort and security.

Depending on your child's needs, a Bedside Buddy Box might include:

★ A glass of water—for those unquenchable thirsts.

★ Favorite books and toys—for those times when your child can't fall asleep.

★ A bathroom pass (see page 39 for details).

★ A flashlight—for checking out mysterious shadows.

★ A cassette player or radio—for the child who feels uncomfortable in a quiet room. (Include a cassette of a parent telling a story or reading a favorite book.)

★ A writing tablet and pencil—for jotting down concerns, problems, or fears that might be keeping your child awake.

★ Something belonging to a parent that will provide comfort to an anxious child—glove, handkerchief, scarf. (Hint: spray with parent's favorite cologne or perfume.)

★ Tissues.

★ A clock.

When choosing items for the Bedside Buddy Box you have to take into consideration your child's age and your wishes as a parent. Perhaps you are comfortable leaving a flashlight and water, but don't want to permit reading or listening to tapes after lights out. There are no hard and fast rules here. The goal of a Bedside Buddy Box is to offer a child alternatives to calling out to parents in the night.

Bedtime Problems

SUGGESTIONS AND SOLUTIONS

If you follow the suggestions in this book for developing a bedtime routine, and follow that routine every night, many of your child's bedtime problems will disappear. But there are some common nighttime problems that a well-structured bedtime routine may not solve.

The solutions to some of these nighttime problems will require your child to change his or her present behavior. Your child may resist these changes. Don't be upset if you have several bad nights before you see a gradual change for the better. This is perfectly normal, but it can be upsetting. Just remember, don't give in. You are teaching your child new habits that will make everyone's bedtime a more pleasant experience.

Here are suggestions for resolving some common nightime problems.

My child is anxious at bedtime.

If you suspect that your child is resisting going to bed because of some anxiety or fear, talk to your child. Try to discover the root of the problem and then take steps to remedy the situation. Follow these six problem-solving steps to help you identify the source of nighttime anxieties and find possible solutions.

1. Bring up the situation that is creating problems at bedtime.

Every night when I tell you it's time to get ready for bed, you argue with me. Instead of going to your bedroom, getting out your pajamas and going to the bathroom to wash up, you argue and beg to stay up.

2. Identify the problem by asking about any fears, anxieties or concerns that make your child unwilling to go to bed.

Why do you argue about going to bed every night? What is it about going to bed that makes you unhappy (angry, fearful)?

3. Ask what could be done differently that might stop the problem. Discuss several plans.

What could you and I do differently that might help you feel more comfortable (safe, happy) when bedtime comes?

You mentioned that you would feel better about going to bed if you didn't have to worry about waking up in the middle of the night in your dark room. What could we do so that you wouldn't be frightened when you wake up in the middle of the night?

4. Choose the plan you and your child agree may work the best.

You mentioned that you would like to sleep with a light on, your bedroom door open and the hall light on, or that you'd like to get a dinosaur night light. Do you think leaving your bedroom lamp on might make your room too bright? The hall light is quite bright, too. Do you think it might keep others awake? What do you think of getting the dinosaur night light and leaving your bedroom door open?

5. Try the plan for a week.

I think that's a great decision. Let's buy that dinosaur night light this afternoon and plug it in. When I turn out your light tonight, the dinosaur night light will shine. And I'll remember to leave your bedroom door open. How does that sound? Let's try it for a week. Every night that you go to bed without arguing or being upset, I'll put a star on your Good Night Chart (see pages 67–68). When you have earned three stars on your chart, you'll get to stay up 30 minutes later on Friday night. If you earn five stars for the week, I'll rent a special video for us to watch on Friday.

6. At the end of the week, decide how the plan is working.

If your child is going to bed without fuss and bother, the solution worked. Continue rewarding your child's good bedtime behavior with lots of praise and a bevy of enthusiastic hugs and kisses. If your child's behavior hasn't improved, try another solution or go through the problem-solving process again. Your child may not have revealed all the concerns and fears that are keeping him awake at night.

BEDTIME PROBLEM

My child gets out of bed many times.

Getting out of bed is an especially common tactic among young children and is usually their way of demanding extra attention. If you follow a bedtime routine as described in this book, your child should have enough of your undivided attention at the end of the day to feel satisfied. But some children are a bit more demanding than others. With these kids, you'll need a little extra ammunition to win the battle. Here are some ideas for preventing some getting-out-of-bed problems by planning for them before they occur.

- **Does your child get out of bed, complaining that she's just not tired?** You cannot force your child to fall asleep, but you can insist that she be in bed at a certain hour. Keep her in bed and occupied by providing her with a few books, one special toy or stuffed animal, and a cassette of soothing music or lullabies—conveniently stored in a decorated Bedtime Buddy Box next to her bed. (See pages 33–34 for specific details.) If your child stalls going to bed for an hour or two every night, complaining that she's not tired, rethink her bedtime. She may require less sleep time than you think. Delay her bedtime for 30–60 minutes for the next few nights to see if the problems continue.

- **Does your child pop out of bed for drinks of water?** Anticipate her requests by putting a glass of water near her bed. Explain that she may not ask for any more water when the glass is empty. Reward a week of following instructions by letting her decorate her very own Bedtime Hour mug.

- **Does your child make numerous trips to the bathroom?** Make sure that a trip to the toilet is the last activity before the lights are turned off, and don't give your child liquids after a certain hour. In addition, create a "Bathroom Pass" for your child. If your child needs to use the bathroom after "lights out," he must give the pass to you on his trip to the toilet. On those nights that your child does not use the pass, he is awarded stars on a chart. When he earns two or three stars, he is rewarded with a special privilege. (If your child is ill, has kidney or bowel problems, or is a chronic bedwetter, you will have to make allowances.)

My child is afraid of the dark.

Fear of the dark is a problem that most children out-grow, but it can be very upsetting to children who are genuinely fearful and are forced by parents to sleep in total darkness. Follow these seven problem-solving steps to help your child.

1. The simplest solution is to leave a light on in the bedroom.

    The light should not be so bright that it will keep your child awake. Your best bet is a night light, but if your child is not comforted by its dim glow, simply reduce the wattage of the bulb in her lamp. A 25-watt bulb (especially a pastel) provides more than enough light to illuminate a child's room. The light should not be a distraction. Move it out of your child's line of sight when your child is lying in bed.

2. Ask your child what she is afraid of.

    Children who are afraid of the dark often fear that something they cannot see is lurking in the room or outside the window. These "shadow monsters" and "closet goblins" can keep your child from getting to sleep if you don't talk about the fears.

    "Why are you crying, dear?"

3. Acknowledge her feelings. Assure her that you will always keep her safe.

    "I can see that you are frightened of some-thing you think is in the closet, so let's check it

out. My job is making sure that you are safe, all the time."

4. Make a physical inspection of the room.

"Let's look in the closet together. I don't see any monsters in there. I see dresses and blouses and coats and shoes. When the light is off in the closet, these clothes don't look the same. Maybe they look like monsters to you. I'm sure that must be the reason because monsters are just make-believe."

5. Make a change in the room that allows your child to feel more comfortable.

"Let's close the closet door and open your bedroom door. The clothes won't look like monsters if the closet door is closed."

6. Assure your child that you are close by.

"Remember, just call me if you get frightened again."

7. Make room inspection part of the Bedtime Hour routine.

If your child's fears continue, he needs more reassurance of his safety. As part of your bedtime routine, inspect the entire room—under the bed, behind the door, in the closet. Check that all windows are locked. Just knowing that everything is safe and sound will have a calming effect on your child.

My child doesn't want to sleep in his own bed.

Most parents at one time or another, have allowed a child to sleep with them. This usually happens when a child has been sick or frightened by a nightmare. But on a nightly basis, this is not a healthy habit to get into. Children need to sleep in their own beds. They need to know that they can be safe and secure at night, away from their parents. If your child is in the habit of slipping into your bed in the middle of the night, then try these suggestions.

1. Prevent the problem before it begins.

    Don't allow the habit to start. If your child is sick and you feel uncomfortable leaving her alone, sleep in her room. If your child is awakened by a nightmare, go to his room and help him get back to sleep. Make sleeping in one's own bedroom a household rule.

2. If your child comes into your room return him to his room immediately.

    As you tuck him in say, "This is your room and this is where you sleep. Good night." Don't make a big fuss. Your child may be tenacious and return several more times. Don't relent and let him in bed with you. Each time you take him back to his room, do it more quietly and firmly than before. Let him know that you are in control and that you won't change your mind, no matter how many times he attempts to gain entry to your bed.

3. Give your child a bedtime buddy.

   Choose one of your child's stuffed animals and tell your child that this is his "bedtime buddy." Now your child has someone to share his bed with, someone to tell secrets to, someone to fall asleep with.

4. Give your child a parent "substitute."

   Give a younger child one of your gloves, handkerchiefs, scarves or old T-shirts to bond with in bed. Just holding on this article will have a comforting effect on your little "bed hopper."

5. Reward your child's progress.

   Use the "Good Night Chart" on pages 67–68 to plot your child's nightly progress. Award your child a point for each night that he sleeps in his own bed. When he has accumulated three points, award him a special privilege. After a week of solo sleeping, give him the special "P.S. I Love You" coupon on pages 69–70. Always remember to praise your child for his efforts.

If problems persist...

✔ You've planned a bedtime routine for your child.

✔ You've tried different techniques to help your child settle down before bed.

✔ You're confident that more serious problems aren't causing your child's bedtime problems.

And yet bedtime is still a battle.

In spite of all the steps you take, sometimes children just want to test your limits—to see if you really mean what you say. Your child is involved in a power struggle with you over bedtime—and you have determined that anxieties or fears are not the problem—and you don't know what to do.

...it's time for a Bedtime Contract.

A Bedtime Contract is a written agreement between you and your child that states:

1. The bedtime rule your child must follow.

2. The specific reward your child will receive for following the bedtime rule.

Bedtime Contract

The new rule in our house will be:

_____
New Rule

If _____
Child's Name

does follow the rule,

_____
Reward

If _____
Child's Name

does not follow the rule,

_____
Consequence

Parent's Signature _____

Child's Signature _____

Date _____

3. The privileges that will be taken away if your child chooses not to follow the rule.

Follow these steps for establishing the rules, rewards and consequences you will use in the contract.

1. Establish the rules for bedtime.

Meet with your child to discuss the specific problem. Explain that there is going to be a new bedtime rule in the house. Depending on the problem your child is having, the new rule may be:

- Start the bedtime routine by a certain time.
- Take care of all nightly hygiene responsibilities.
- Gather belongings for the next day.
- Turn lights out by a certain time.
- Stay in bed once lights are out.
- Other_____

Say to your child, for example:

> *"Nicole, we've already tried several things to help you get to bed on time so you will to get the sleep you need, but we're still having problems. We have to solve this because you are overtired in the morning. Most days you can barely get up. What we are going to do is have a new bedtime rule. The new rule is this: You will begin getting ready for bed at 8:00. Lights will be out at 8:45."*

Write the new rule on the Bedtime Contract (pages 71–72).

2. Establish the rewards for following the rules.

Your goal is for your child to be successful with the new rule, and to get the sleep he or she needs. Offer your child an incentive. For example, each night your child chooses to follow the rule, he or she may:

- Earn a sticker or star on the Good Night Chart (pages 67–68).

- Earn extra "stay up" time on the weekend.

- Watch a favorite "before bed" video with Mom or Dad the next night.

- Earn extra story reading time with Mom or Dad.

- Earn five minutes of music in bed.

- Other_____

Say to your child, for example:

> *"I know that you can follow this rule, Nicole—I know you can start getting ready for bed on time and be in bed on time. And to let you know how much I appreciate it, every night that you follow the rule, you will earn a star on your Good Night Chart. When you have five stars, you will earn the privilege of staying up an hour later on Saturday night."*

Write the reward on the Bedtime Contract (pages 71–72).

3. Establish the consequences if the rules are not followed.

Decide what privilege or activity you will take away if your child does not follow the new rule. For example, your child might:

- Lose the privilege of playing with friends after school the next day.
- Lose telephone privileges the next day.
- Have to go to his or her bedroom earlier the next night.
- Lose radio or stereo privileges.
- Other_____

Say to your child, for example:

> *"If you don't choose to follow the rule, you'll lose a privilege. That means each night that you do not begin getting ready for bed on time, and turn the lights out on time, you will have to spend the evening in your room after dinner. No TV. No radio.*

> *"Nicole, it's important for your health and it's important if you are to do your best in school. I hope you will choose to follow this rule because I love you and I want what's best for you."*

Write the consequence on the Bedtime Contract (pages 71–72).

Sign the contract and date it.

Remember, you must be consistent:

- If your child breaks the rule, you must follow through with the consequence.

- If your child follows the rule, you must provide the reward.

- Praise your child whenever he or she follows the rule.

How to Speak

SO YOUR CHILD WILL LISTEN

Does your child tune you out, ignore you, or argue with you when you ask him or her to get ready for bed (or anything else for that matter)? If this is typical in your home it may have a lot to do with the way you are speaking to your child.

Parents who are successful in encouraging better behavior speak to their children in a clear, direct and firm manner that leaves no doubt about what is expected.

Parents who are ignored or argued with often speak in a way that is either wishy-washy or hostile.

Do any of these comments sound familiar?

"How many times do I have to remind you to brush your teeth?"

"Please take your bath. It's already nine-thirty."

"It's past your bedtime and you haven't even finished your homework."

"Why do you always have to wait until the last minute to tell me that you need a check for tomorrow?"

Chances are you've said things like these many times. Most parents have. But what do statements like these really say to your child? Look at each statement carefully and you will see that they either ask pointless questions, beg, or make an obvious statement of fact. They do not let the child know without a doubt that you expect her to brush her teeth, take her bath, do her homework earlier or get organized for the next day. Wishy-washy statements don't let your child know that your words are to be taken seriously—that you mean business.

They make it easy for your child to ignore you.

And what about comments like these?

"I should know better than expect you to brush your teeth without being told a million times."

"You can't take your bath when you're supposed to? Then maybe you should just go to school dirty."

"That's it. You can just stay home this weekend."

What do these all-too-common remarks say to a child? Put-downs, meaningless threats and off-the-wall punishments, because they are emotional and often inappropriate, are an invitation to challenge and anger. Because they disregard a child's feelings they send a message to a child that says "I don't like you." Hostile responses tear down a child's self-esteem and are ultimately damaging. The words your child hears from you will become the way he feels about himself.

Learn to speak so your child will listen.

Don't beg. Don't get angry. Don't become exasperated. Instead, when making a request of your child, be calm and use direct statements that send your child this message: "This is what I expect you to do."

> *"Audrey, time to get ready for bed. Start your bath now."*

> *"Marco, go brush your teeth now."*

> *"Chris, Put your dirty clothes in the hamper."*

Confident, clear and direct statements get results.

And if your child argues?

Above all, don't argue back. Do not get involved in a discussion. It will get you nowhere. The following scene illustrates this point:

Parent: *Carlos, time to get ready for bed.*

Child: (playing a video game) *I'm not tired yet. Just let me get to the next level. I'm almost there.*

Parent: *Carlos, you've been sitting in front of that game for hours. Now please get ready for bed.*

Child: *You're so unfair. I said I'm almost at the next level. This is farther than I've ever been before.*

Parent:	*You always say that. Can't you just do what I ask for once?*
Child:	*Hold on. It doesn't mater if I go to bed now or in a few minutes.*
Parent:	*Carlos, you keep this arguing up and I will get rid of that machine. I've told you that before and I really mean it.*

What happened here? By arguing—by getting into a pointless discussion—the parent has lost control of the situation. Carlos is still playing the video game. And the frustrated parent resorted to meaningless threats that Carlos has heard many times. Threats that have never been carried out! What should you do in a situation like this?

Don't argue. Use the "broken record" technique.

First, very clearly tell your child what you want him to do. If he argues, simply repeat the statement, like a broken record. Do not argue back or even discuss the issue. Repeat your expectation.

For example:

Parent:	*Carlos, time to get ready for bed.*
Child:	(playing a video game) *I'm not tired yet. Just let me get to the next level. I'm almost there.*

Parent:	*I understand that you may not be tired, but it's time to get ready for bed. Turn the game off now.*
Child:	*You're so unfair. I said I'm almost at the next level. This is farther than I've ever been before.*
Parent:	*I understand that you want to continue playing Carlos, but you need to turn off the game and get ready for bed now.*

By staying firm, not arguing, not getting sidetracked, chances are good your child will comply with your request. He or she may grumble and complain, but will probably get up and do as you ask.

If necessary, back up your words with actions.

If, however, after three repetitions of your expectations your child still does not comply, it's time to back up your words with actions and present your child with a clear choice:

Parent:	*Carlos, I expect you to turn off the game and get ready for bed, now. If you choose not to get ready for bed you will choose to lose the use of the video system for the entire next week. The choice is yours.*

By giving your child a choice, you place responsibility for what happens right where it belongs—squarely on your child's shoulders.

Try these techniques the next time your child balks at fulfilling a responsibility or responding to a request. Just take a deep breath and follow through calmly and confidently. You'll find that this approach does work!

Parents Want to Know

Q & A

Bedtime should be the peaceful beginning to a much-needed night's sleep. We all need adequate sleep to perform our best during the day. And as parents we know how important a good night's sleep is to a growing child. But problems often arise at bedtime that make the trip to dreamland a stressful, anxious, and sometimes uncooperative journey.

Here are some common concerns about bedtime from parents just like you.

Question: *Our six-year-old son is a perpetual motion machine who just hates to go to bed. He doesn't seem tired at his bedtime so my husband and I often let him stay up later with us. Just how much sleep should a six-year-old boy have each night?*

Answer: A child of six usually requires from 10 to 11 hours of sleep per day. This, however, can vary from child to child depending on his sleep needs. If your child is still taking naps, shorten or stop them for a week to see if your son is more tired at bedtime. It is very important to start your son on a regular bedtime routine as soon as possible. Set a bedtime and make sure that you spend "quality time" tucking him in, talking about the day and reading to him. This special one-on-one time gives your son the reassurance and comfort that makes these nightly separations easier to handle.

Question: *This problem may seem trivial, but it's driving my husband and me crazy. As soon as we put our five-year-old daughter to bed, she calls out for a drink of water. Sometimes she'll ask for three or four glasses before we finally put a stop to it. What can we do?*

Answer: The first glass of water may have been a genuine request to quench a bedtime thirst. But the other requests were probably attention-getting devices. First, place a glass of water on a table by your daughter's bed. Secondly, post a "Good Night" chart (pages 67–68) on your child's bedroom wall. Explain that for every evening she does not ask for a drink of water (or make any other unnecessary requests), you will place a star on her chart. When she has earned three stars, she will receive a special prize. Always remember to praise your daughter in the morning for good bedtime behavior.

Question: *How important is reading to a child at bedtime? My daughter loves to hear stories, but sometimes there just isn't enough time. Any suggestions?*

Answer: Educators agree that reading aloud to children is the single most important activity parents can do to help children become successful readers. Reading aloud will improve your daughter's listening skills, expand her vocabulary, awaken her curiosity, spark her imagination, and give her a strong foundation for language. It also provides a special opportunity for you and your child to share the world that can only be created through the written word—without television, without videos, without computers. Considering how important reading aloud can be to your child academically, you should spend at least 5 to 10 minutes each evening reading special books and stories to her. On the weekends, you can increase the read-aloud time when you aren't as overwhelmed by weeknight demands.

Question: *My seven-year-old son is afraid of the dark. How can I break him of this fear?*

Answer: Fear of the dark is very common among children. Young imaginations can conjure up all sorts of monsters and night creatures once Mom and Dad have tucked their children in and the lights are turned out. First and foremost, your child needs reassurance from you that everything is all right. During the daytime, talk about what he fears when the lights are out. Ask him what would make him feel more safe and secure at night. Studies have shown that there is no real advantage to forcing your child to sleep in the dark, so leave on a night light or lamp with a low-wattage bulb.

Question: *My eight-year-old daughter still takes her security blanket to bed with her. Is this normal?*

Answer: Many children rely on special toys or animals for comfort and security at bedtime. If cuddling with her favorite blanket gives your child reassurance and helps her fall asleep easily and get a good night's sleep, then let her use it.

Question: *Every night it's the same old story. I try to get my ten-year-old to bed and he begs for "just one more show!" Sometimes I say OK, sometimes I don't, but either way we have an argument and he ends up going to bed an hour or so later than I'd like.*

Answer: Without a doubt, TV can be the toughest part of bedtime for most families. Children always want "just one more show," and parents are often too tired at night to say no. The trouble is, once you make an exception ("All right. You can watch another show, but just for tonight.") you set the stage for arguments every night. Once your child knows you might back down, he'll try it as often as he likes. And most often, it works. The answer? Once you set a bedtime for your child, stand your ground. (See pages 49–54 for tips on how to speak to your child.) Your child needs adequate sleep, and neither of you need arguments. You might also consider setting some TV rules, too. Let your child pick one or two shows each night to watch (within the time frame you choose). Explain that once his choices have been viewed, that's it for TV that night. Doing this will help your child learn to choose specific programs he wants to see rather than just watch anything (and everything) that's on.

Top 10
Reminders

Your better bedtime routine is under way and the battles are winding down. With your continued attention, and adjustments as your child grows older, nighttimes can continue to be one of the best parts of the day. Here then are our top ten "bedtime battles" reminders to help you keep things on track and running smoothly. Refer to these reminders from time to time whenever you need a quick refresher!

1. A better next day for your child begins with getting enough sleep. Set an appropriate bedtime for your child and stick to it. Bedtime arguments often occur when children know they can bargain for "just another half hour." It's hard not to give in, but adequate sleep is important for your child, and avoiding nightly arguments is important for you.

2. Personal hygiene, consisting of washing, brushing and flossing, must become a regular part of your child's nighttime routine. The habits your child learns while young will likely become habits adopted for a lifetime.

3. Your mornings will be less stressful for everyone if you and your child make some next-day preparations the night before. Choosing clothes, gathering homework and school supplies, and packing lunches are all activities that can be taken care of at night—relieving your overburdened mornings of a little bit of pressure.

4. Whenever possible, your child's nighttime routine should include special time shared by both of you. Reading a story, talking about the day's events, sharing thoughts—just spending time together—will give your child a calm, secure ending to the day, resulting in better sleep and a better tomorrow.

5. It's important to structure weeknight bedtimes so that your child knows exactly what time to be in bed each night—and gets enough sleep. While you don't want to deviate too much from this schedule on the weekend, you can allow your child a bit more flexibility then. Many parents find that offering a later bedtime on weekends as a reward for getting to bed on time during the week will motivate kids to stay on schedule and avoid arguing.

6. You can count on children to argue occasionally about bedtime, and lots of other issues, too. When your child doesn't cooperate with your requests, don't argue and don't beg for compliance. Stay firm. Calmly state your expectations, and repeat them if necessary. Don't get involved in pointless arguments or defensive discussions. Standing your ground will lead to a happier bedtime for all.

7. As bedtime approaches, your child's activities should become quieter and calmer. Sleep will come more easily if your child has an opportunity to wind down from the day's more strenuous activities. Quiet music, a board game or reading is a better prelude to slumber than roughhousing, intense TV or video games.

8. It's easy to take good behavior for granted yet quickly pounce on inappropriate behavior. Turn this tendency around. Look for opportunities to praise your child for cooperating at bedtime. Your praise will encourage your child to continue the good behavior.

9. As every parent knows, in spite of everything you do, some problems just aren't easily solved. Keep in mind that it's to your benefit, and to your child's, to actively help him or her make better behavior choices. A bedtime contract (as described in this book) will give you the structure you sometimes need to get your child on track.

10. Consider your child's nighttime routine with yourself in mind, too. Another good reason for your child to have a reasonable, consistent bedtime is to give you some time for yourself, your spouse or your own interests. If you provide your child with a pleasant bedtime routine (that includes spending time with you) you can feel good about taking the time you deserve for yourself at the end of a busy day.

Bedtime Hour Worksheets

PLANNING SHEETS, CHARTS AND NOTES

On the following pages are the worksheets that were introduced in this book. (You may want to enlarge them so that they are easier to fill in.) Make additional copies before using so there will always be an ample supply on hand.

2-Week Sleep Diary

Bedtime Hour Chart

Good Night Chart

P.S. I Love You Coupons

Bedtime Contract

2-Week
Sleep Diary
Week 1

DAY 1
Woke up: _____ Went to bed: _____
Comments: _____
_____

DAY 2
Woke up: _____ Went to bed: _____
Comments: _____
_____

DAY 3
Woke up: _____ Went to bed: _____
Comments: _____
_____

DAY 4
Woke up: _____ Went to bed: _____
Comments: _____
_____

DAY 5
Woke up: _____ Went to bed: _____
Comments: _____
_____

DAY 6
Woke up: _____ Went to bed: _____
Comments: _____
_____

DAY 7
Woke up: _____ Went to bed: _____
Comments: _____
_____

2-Week
Sleep Diary
Week 2

DAY
8
Woke up: _____ Went to bed: _____
Comments: _____
_____
_____

DAY
9
Woke up: _____ Went to bed: _____
Comments: _____
_____
_____

DAY
10
Woke up: _____ Went to bed: _____
Comments: _____
_____
_____

DAY
11
Woke up: _____ Went to bed: _____
Comments: _____
_____
_____

DAY
12
Woke up: _____ Went to bed: _____
Comments: _____
_____
_____

DAY
13
Woke up: _____ Went to bed: _____
Comments: _____
_____
_____

DAY
14
Woke up: _____ Went to bed: _____
Comments: _____
_____
_____

BEDTIME HOUR
Chart

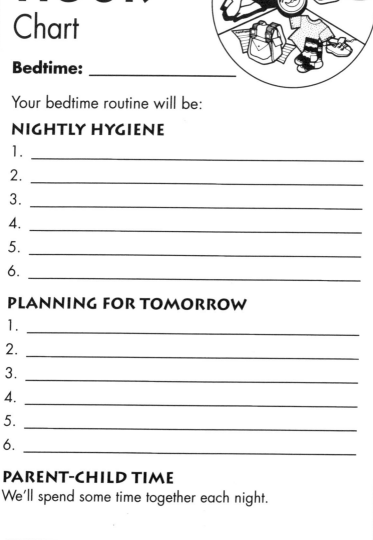

Bedtime: _____

Your bedtime routine will be:

NIGHTLY HYGIENE

1. _____
2. _____
3. _____
4. _____
5. _____
6. _____

PLANNING FOR TOMORROW

1. _____
2. _____
3. _____
4. _____
5. _____
6. _____

PARENT-CHILD TIME
We'll spend some time together each night.

_____
Parent Signature

BEDTIME HOUR
Chart

Bedtime: _____

Your bedtime routine will be:

NIGHTLY HYGIENE

1. _____
2. _____
3. _____
4. _____
5. _____
6. _____

PLANNING FOR TOMORROW

1. _____
2. _____
3. _____
4. _____
5. _____
6. _____

PARENT-CHILD TIME
We'll spend some time together each night.

_____
Parent Signature

GOOD NIGHT!
Chart

WHEN I EARN _____ STARS,

I WILL RECEIVE _____.

Parents: Every night that your child behaves appropriately, draw a star on the chart. Younger children earn the reward in a few days, older children in one week. A special reward may also be earned after receiving a specified number of stars in a month.

GOOD NIGHT!
Chart

WHEN I EARN _____ STARS,

I WILL RECEIVE _____.

Parents: Every night that your child behaves appropriately, draw a star on the chart. Younger children earn the reward in a few days, older children in one week. A special reward may also be earned after receiving a specified number of stars in a month.

Thanks!

_____

❤ P.S. I Love You!

Great Night!

_____

❤ P.S. I Love You!

Sweet Dreams!

_____

❤ P.S. I Love You!

Use these coupons to write a caring note to your child or to present a special reward.

69

Sweet Dreams!

_____

P.S. I Love You!

Great Night!

_____

P.S. I Love You!

Thanks!

_____

P.S. I Love You!

Use these coupons to write a caring note to your child or to present a special reward.

Bedtime Contract

The new rule in our house will be:

_____
New Rule

If _____
Child's Name

does follow the rule,

_____
Reward

_____

If _____
Child's Name

does not follow the rule,

_____
Consequence

_____

_____
Parent's Signature

_____
Child's Signature

_____
Date

Bedtime Contract

The new rule in our house will be:

_____
New Rule

If _____
Child's Name

does follow the rule,

_____
Reward

_____

If _____
Child's Name

does not follow the rule,

_____
Consequence

_____

_____
Parent's Signature

_____
Child's Signature

_____
Date